# The Life You Gave Me

# The Life You Gave Me

Poems by

Claire Drucker

© 2023 Claire Drucker. All rights reserved.
This material may not be reproduced in any form, published,
reprinted, recorded, performed, broadcast,
rewritten or redistributed without
the explicit permission of Claire Drucker.
All such actions are strictly prohibited by law.

Cover design by Annie Danberg

ISBN: 978-1-63980-444-3

Kelsay Books
502 South 1040 East, A-119
American Fork, Utah 84003
Kelsaybooks.com

*To my grandmother, Ella (Omi),
and to my mother, Anneliese, who loved me with all of their might.
To my grandfather, Hermann, whose death gave my life breath.
And to my daughter, Gracie,
the greatest gift of this lifetime.*

*A big thank you to my sister, Julie,
and my dear ones, especially Nance, Jenny, Annie,
Jen, Shan, Joel, and Stacy,
who cheered me on tirelessly over the years.*

*An extra special shout-out to Annie Danberg for her amazing
cover design
and to Carolyn Clark, whose editing helped shape this book
you hold in your hands.*

*And last but not least,
to the Great Mother of us all.*

# Acknowledgments

Thank you to the following publications, where versions of these poems previously appeared:

*Autumn Sky Poetry:* "Pantoum"

*CA Quarterly:* "Exile"

*The Freedom of New Beginnings:* "Ode to Resilience"

*Home: One Word, Many Stories:* "Ode to the Tiny House"

*The Jewish Literary Journal:* "Third Day of Hanukkah"

*Rust & Moth:* "Great Blue Heron," "The Life You Gave Me"

*Young Ravens Literary Review:* "The Dying Time," "Back to the Wild"

# Contents

His Name     13

I. The Body Will Remember

Dear America     17
Alternative Facts     19
Walk     21
The Pledge     22
If Discrimination Suddenly Became Extinct     24

II. As If We Were Birds

Apple Juicing     27
Forever Red     29
Orr Hot Springs     30
Dancing on this Sunday Morning     31
Winter Storm     32
Pantoum     33
Deeper the World Burns     34

III. Umbilical

Umbilical     37
Source     39
The Wall Between     41
Tethered     42
From the Shore     43
Day at Pinnacle Gulch     44
Growing Up     45
Ode to the Tiny House     47
Soprano of Our Singing     48

IV. Future On A Pillow

The New Season                                51
Tubbs Fire, 2017                              52
What If                                       53
Months Later, What Remains                    54
Camp Fire                                     55
In the DMV                                    56

V. Build Me a Mountain

New Year's 2020, B.C. (Before Covid)          59
Exile                                         60
End of Days                                   61
Escape                                        62
What Was Once a Street                        63
After Lockdown                                64
Back to the Wild                              65
Ode to Resilience                             66

VI. If Not for His Hands

The Life You Gave Me                          69
Great Blue Heron                              70
Saying No to Treatment                        71
Apple Valley Skilled Nursing                  73
Don't Turn the Light On                       75
The Beast                                     78

## VII. You Won't Forget Me

| | |
|---|---|
| Mishegas | 81 |
| Look Harder | 83 |
| Morphine Hell | 85 |
| Like A Miracle | 87 |
| Release Me | 89 |

## VIII. The Leaving Place

| | |
|---|---|
| Mushrooming at Salt Point | 93 |
| The Promise | 94 |
| Third Day of Hanukkah | 96 |
| The Dying Time | 98 |
| The Sound of You | 100 |
| Disorientation | 101 |
| Unravelling | 103 |
| You Are Not a Mountain | 104 |

# His Name

*for my grandfather*

At 32, I found his last words in my mother's closet,
bottom of a cardboard box next to winter coats and socks.

To be Jewish in 1938 Vienna was to know denial
that kept them sleepless, hoping it would pass.

America had turned her back on his Romanian birthplace,
bolted the lock, sealed with a final shove.

My grandfather researched for months, telling no one
while Nazis marched their brown boots down the streets

and his daughter, my mother, cried in her sleep,
not too young to taste fear.

Like so many, he lost his work, his money, his God.
He left the note on the wooden table, said he loved them always,

why he had to free them, himself, without his life
he knew they had a chance to flee. To re-make time.

White enamel oven and the tick of the clock.
His own shaking hand on the black dial.

Sacrifice   *to suffer someone to be lost*
*to offer something up, for the sacred.*

After he died, my grandmother begged
the consulate's wife on her knees, for visas,

for any kind of kindness. She sailed on the Normandie
with her two small children, a handful

of refugees in the hold, while the wealthy
toasted their luck with champagne

and for decades, they never spoke his name:
Hermann, inventor with the soft eyelids

and generous heart, who battled depression after
the Great War, the one she said was too good

for this world. If not for his hands on that cool knob
I would not be here, giving something up,

telling all of you this story.

# I.

# The Body Will Remember

# Dear America

The diagnosis is in, and the prognosis does not look good.
You have a cancer in the heart, half of your white cells
are eating the others alive, gnawing away at kindness
and the small bones of generosity, leaving a sour taste
of bile, a liver that wants to dominate the equality
coursing through you, the ones that threaten
to choke the marrow you are made of.

Dear America, you have always been less than healthy.
Smoking tobacco tainted with the bloody whip
of scars and the smell of terror, drinking
too much cheap whiskey from the stolen land
of corn and squash where the grandmothers prayed.
The songs of children enslaved in your nightmares at 3am
when even the mockingbird could not find a reason to sing.
Of overeating a fatty feast of misogyny
served by adolescent girls in see-through skirts, begging
for a morsel, a crumb, because they were starved
for any kind of chance to know who they really were.

So now, America, it has come to this. Again. Fear
and bigotry have infected your lungs with a greasy smut made
from selfish desires, given you a tumor of enormous proportions.
This malignancy does not read books, does not know your dreams
or the spirit of your constitution. This tumor tastes only of hate,
eats the green hemp to grow fat on white supremacy.
This foul-smelling blot who should be jailed for raping
but instead crouches at the helm of your body, venomous
tendrils, those fat sticky fingers on the button of your existence.

You cannot run from this one. It will turn your skin into an oozing
yellow mass of complacency, eat away the truth of what
you have tried not to see. It will weaken the tissue of your
intestines, the place where justice lives, until you are crawling
around on your knees, blind with a suffering no illusion can erase.

But within your lands, America, there is a place, a glance,
a small sound like running water,
another well deep within the well of holy ground,
a way you might be saved after all.

Come close.
It is a quiet humming
embedded in the mitochondria of goodness.
A possibility of hope inching toward the nucleus of your future.
Migrants, artists, mothers, dancers, clowns, come out to the edges
of this river, this expanse of canyon sage and red sand,
to speak the silence hidden in the stone of your lives.

Come closer.
Talk truth, draw a circle in the dirt, lay hands
on each other's backs.
Capture the wind flying through the streets.
Come with your fists raised, your appetites on fire.
Eat the apple of rebellion, write
your stories on the wings of ravens.
Come as you are, with your imperfect smiles
and your delicate needs

but never never
stop reaching
for the true democracy
prophesied
in dreams.

Maybe then, dear America, you can finally be free.

# Alternative Facts

My students question assumptions—
why don't we shift our lifestyle knowing
the climate crisis will hasten the downfall,
how can people slow the heating earth.

But wait, that didn't happen—
those students sit like robots under fluorescent
lights, questioning nothing, warming's only
temporary, a hoax, it's important
to believe alternative facts.

I talk to my grandmother, dead more than 20 years,
who said Americans would never let fascists
into the White House, this could never happen
here.

Hold on now, I don't talk to anyone, nothing
exists except these untruths, forming
and un-forming, rearranging
puzzle pieces, all lies shiny with sweat and dirt.

At night, I run my hands over my girlfriend's
smooth skin, kiss her soft, wet tongue
tasting of cocoa
and mountain air.

Wait, the substitute facts—
she only makes love to cardboard men who
bite like doggies, sniffing crotches
and humping in and out the dry moans
of pale grabbing hands.
We know she loves it.
To say otherwise is a lie.

No students, no survivors, no
lover, no critique,
only the words
coming from this mouth are real.
Listen,
everything else is bad.
Only alternative facts are good.

I bow to the women
who came before
and before them and before them,
the ones who listened and the ones who did not.

I gather my daughter, my sister, my family,
my friends, my students, my community, my people,
this democracy, this world
into my arms and tell them about love,

hard scraping eat-your-heart-out-love.
I tattoo the events, the grief, the beauty of every moment
into my skin, so when the tsunami sweeps it away,
my body will remember
the truth of what was said.

# Walk

*for all parents who have lost children to gun violence*

Walk your child to school while they
wonder about ice cream, chocolate or cherry
with the marshmallows, *can we get some later*

*after homework?* Walk them through the light,
then the stop sign on the next corner, the one
with the "s" blacked out spelling "top."

Walk through early morning heat as you think
about what to make for dinner,
spaghetti or tamales or chicken quesadillas,

past the same man asking for money
so he can buy himself a sandwich
or a beer, his home, a box, a dog.

Walk up the front steps, open the metal
door, bend down and kiss your child
on the cheek, feel their love as they wrap

their arms around your neck.

Walk to the living room, to your phone, to the call,
that moment when time died a slow, repeating death.

Now walk backwards to the start of the day
again and again, as if you could un-peel it, as if
you could unfasten the moment and throw it

anywhere but here, walk as if you could keep
those arms pressed around your neck
forever.

# The Pledge

I pledge allegiance to the hippies and artists in coastal
California, the ones drawing murals, raising chickens, star

gazing, to the rainbow flag dazzling with light, to the dykes,
their soft breasts and tough biceps, wishing they could
take a shot at—as they march in peaceful demonstrations.
I pledge allegiance to the earthworms,

and the bees, to the children in the school
yard who have to worry for their lives, the ones
who know what respect actually smells like. I pledge

my heart to the earth-stained creases
on a grandmother's brown face, her hands toughened
like a saint. I pledge my spirit to the ones whose land, language
and dreams were stolen again and again, to the state
of oneness with all living beings
of compassion
and laughter
of everyone gets a living wage, clean water.

I pledge myself to the republic of love and generosity,
for which it stands
in a circle holding each other up, giving thanks
for being alive
on this earth heating up, spinning into oblivion,

one nation under the Great Mother
who should agree to disagree but politely
and with integrity. I pledge allegiance
to the families struggling to pay
rent, put food on the table
under a dog is my co-pilot banner
(wait, she left town, couldn't stand the racist policies,
now she's on Machu Picchu, praying for the vulnerable).

Coast to coast, indivisible, especially now, a pledge
for understanding, so if I looked
into your eyes you wouldn't ship me off
to become straighter
than a road in Nevada
but take me in your arms and say, *I'm one too.*
With liberty and remembrance for all who fought,

I pledge kindness
I pledge justice for history's transgressions
I pledge to stand against suffering
with forgiveness
under a big moon, in silence,
with freedom and goodness
for all.

# If Discrimination Suddenly Became Extinct

If discrimination suddenly became extinct, children would leap out of detention camps and into the arms of their mothers, who are now stakeholders in all of the Fortune 500s. The single mother on welfare would kneel on the floor in disbelief with a check big enough to buy a house in Marin, for all the work she lost from staying home with her children. The young girl in a wheelchair would roll herself over every beach boardwalk, laughing, her hair flying back and chocolate ice cream at the corners of her mouth. Dinosaurs that had been in hiding would walk up the hills of small towns in Mississippi and bend down to comfort the trans ones who are now free to be you and me, partying in the streets, screaming and crying with joy. Pterodactyls would pick up all the gay folks of color in one fell swoop and carry them to their fantasy vacation spot, all expenses paid for the rest of their lives, where the homophobes and bigots would become their servants, paid poorly and forced to sleep on the cold, hard floor. If discrimination became a thing of yesterday, all of the shoes that had been silent would find their voices and announce that they no longer wanted feet to tread in them. To kill the soul would be outlawed. All the guns would be melted down into trains, so we could get out of our cars and tell our stories. Women everywhere would be the only ones to decide what happens to our bodies, and men would bleed monthly and bear children out of their stomachs. Frogs would get in on it too and disrupt all of the technology, so we'd have to go back to writing letters and meeting at the town square, while hummingbirds would realize it is time to come clean and reveal they are really the present and future Dalai Lamas combined. That if they fly close enough, and look directly into our eyes, our minds would meld and we could become part hummingbird and part mystic, too.

II.

As If We Were Birds

# Apple Juicing

Hands in the depths,
knobby-kneed Gravensteins
submerged and bobbing
in the wooden barrel.
Joel has the mojo,
rolling the smooth wet fruit
over and down in the cold water.
Summer's dance into autumn,
a fifty-year-old tradition, juicing
Sebastopol's abundance like
a cleansing of promises.
A nectar so sweet
you could lie down in it
and weep.

First, throw the red fruit into the press,
listen to the teeth of the beast devouring.
Pulp builds in the wooden bucket lined with mesh,
then stop, switch spots, put the round cover over the mush
and squeeze the goodness again. Walk the long stick around
her metal fingers. *Voila!* Elixir in the stainless steel pan
to be decanted into old milk jugs and mason jars
to get giddy on at home, for baking
or enjoyed hot on a cold winter's night.

Straining at the turning wheel, knees engaged,
in this score, everyone has their job—
tamper, thrower, spinner, wincher, pourer—
even the wasps are doing what they should,
legs sticky with sugar, languid
and drowning in the garnet liquid.

Nathan puns repeatedly as he turns the handle.
Jen and Choz cut out the bruises,
CJ, Ilona, and Josh empty and fill, fill and empty:

water, apples, buckets, life
the old way together.
Laughing banter since
nothing happens without the
others, we lean in with love, for any kind
of freedom, sweaty juice glistening our skin
to a shine in this bamboo forest.
With apple heaven on our lips, we
inhale moon flowers, heat
of the day, honeysuckle fog-blanket.

# Forever Red

*Seneca Falls, 2017*

Smell of summer thunder, lake swims
and bonbon fights, rushing of snowmelt
on canyon shale. Crimson
cherries on their tiny stems,
plucked from trees singing
a sour-sweet melody. We pick
and pick and pick, sweat staining t-shirts,
each thump in the yellow pail,
more and more hearts from
the branches of the sky.
In the lake, floating
in circles, forgetting ourselves with
orange malts, kayaking, the lazy loosening
of the world's threads.
Outside of all routine, we laugh
at what we cannot hold. Oldest
of friends who hear my thoughts,
who almost knows me better than I know myself,
our spirit child, fishing for
perch off the dock, has your blackberry hair.
Her laughter: sun-kissed chocolate days, tapioca
crystals in the bowl, cherry
pie waiting to bake.
To remember every tiny footfall,
to spill the sky into our bodies
as if we were birds.

## Orr Hot Springs

I melt inside honeysuckle,
foxglove, heat of
summer on stone
buddha, a granite fountain
cascading into cold
pool carved by sulfurous waters.
Another tongue for earth's fire.

I ease my body full to bursting
with anxious phone calls,
middle of the night ER visits,
continuous paperwork, into
the mouth of that other Mother,
the one I can still be a child with,
to let her waters empty me of any
sounds I recognize as my own.

I rise from winter to summer, skin
stripped from hypnotic minerals
passing through pores, untethering
from the world, from the smell of myself.
Minutes stretch concave into years,
my heart on the towel, slowed
to just a whisper, slant
of shadow on pouring light.

Sinking into birdsong
molecular conversion
cell by tiny cell,
I disappear beneath the ripples,
only bubbles where my hands reach up
and slice a path through.
Overhead a Doug Fir catches sun's arc,
nothing but a red dragonfly
dancing motionless in the air.

# Dancing on this Sunday Morning

Sorrow breaks us clean in two,
pushes us into tender holds
of fingers, thighs, rolling
patterns of light
in a room listening for the shout of the world.
Quiet in the moments after crash of waves
empties the breath, shock
and awe of being torn open,
then the reach for each other's hearts
deciphering a familiar language, reeling toward
the soft spot on the elbow, a cupped chin,
to standing, an act of courage, the floor liquid
beneath blurred feet, turning and
turning, throwing the weight of ourselves
into any back that will hold us, hurrying into
each other's names
no longer one or the other but bodies
flying through everything, reminding
us again: so this is how to live.

# Winter Storm

*for J.*

froths boats into cream,
small toys in the immensity
of swells lick the sky,
thick with stratus clouds, gray as beginnings
except for a slit where light or angels
bend down to open up the churning mass.
This stretch of sand, bull kelp, and driftwood
almost petrified by wind,
wash through this birthday
like anthropologists from the past
and the two years since cancer made you who you are.
Where does it come from? Where will it go?
Eucalyptus root slid down from Oregon, plastic bottle
from a dump in Washington. The future
vibrates under our legs,
almost swallowed up by the roar of it.
Farther and farther from safety,
we sip our soup, warm in our mouths—

you and me
alive at the same time—
what a tasty joy.

# Pantoum

*for my students*

Words like cherry blossoms, inhale of beginnings,
you agonize over getting it right, your soul there, not there.
I am most myself in the classroom, in the heat of ideas,
root of the maple, branches intertwining toward tomorrow.

You agonize over getting it right, your soul there, not there,
this earth spinning more quickly than it used to,
root of the maple, branches intertwining toward
tomorrow. Every year we had rainy winters that left the gutters

running, this earth spinning more quickly than it used to,
your desire for knowledge, a less constant need than food.
Every year we had rainy winters that left the gutters running.
I want to give you back to yourself, to taste this moment,

your desire for knowledge, a less constant need than food.
Where would you go if you only had a few days left to breathe?
I want to give you back to yourself, to taste this moment, but
sweet, warm air brushes some longing that cannot be named.

Where would you go if you only had a few days left to breathe?
Your hands reach for each other, not for grades or homework.
Sweet, warm air brushes some longing that cannot be named,
I want to give you the moon but the ocean pulls away these days.

Your hands reach for each other, not for grades or homework.
I want to give you the moon but the ocean pulls away these days.
Words like cherry blossoms, inhale of beginnings.
I am most myself in the classroom, in the heat of ideas.

# Deeper the World Burns

*after Mary Oliver's "The Journey"*

Before you, there were
days of cold, dark rain then
white owl, Buddha, bright dust.
You came to tell us how
droplets twisted from veined leaf
reflect stars, seasons, moonlit
threads of thought-water
that catch in the ribs
knowing only what bones know.

Your long slow climb to that pond
where salamanders in their orange
and black wetsuits paddle
slow-motion in the bracken
remind again—impermanence
and its opposite, joy—
how the world can hold all of us at once.
It licks flaming tongues at our feet
gathering all the quiet into syllables,
and still you throw roses into our hair
singing that essential song—
to leave voices behind and find our place
in the round stone, green wave
late or early
here or not
because of you
deeper the world burns
and we tremble

*determined to do the only thing we can do*
*determined to save the only life we can save.*

# III.

# Umbilical

# Umbilical

You carry this kidney bean inside your body, dream of her coming through a doorway surrounded by angels in yellow chiffon, your friend says *isn't being pregnant like being in a state of grace* and you give this kidney bean-turned-eggplant a name, like scientists name trees or grasses and publish them in books. You know you have been given one of the greatest gifts in the world, but when you watch little boys run around the store at top speed, your heart refuses to slow down. You think, *what if I give birth to one of those?*

The midwife says *reach down and pull out your* kidney bean-turned-eggplant-turned watermelon baby and her hand is nestled by the side of her face, as if she's ready to reach up to you, to the world, eyes wide open, dark hair moist from the ride. You and her Dad and her Auntie and her Goddess-mother and even the midwives cry and cry at this miracle so ordinary it is happening thousands of times in every corner of the planet. Then you both sing the welcome song set to the tune of "Fa Hoo Doree" from the TV movie *When the Grinch Stole Christmas* and your baby sleeps on your breast, mouth already moving to find the milk that will sustain her, the food you will make from your blood and daily meat intake, with a few random carrots thrown in because it's California and we're all supposed to eat healthy.

You carry her into the bathroom when you have to pee, you put her in the red and white bouncy seat while you do the mounds of dishes, you try to put her down for a few minutes, into the spot her Dad has dubbed the "kryptonite cradle," but she starts to whimper only a few inches from the sheepskin bottom, so you roll her on the big, green ball in the middle of the night and re-learn all the songs you have forgotten, particularly *inchworm, inchworm, measuring the marigolds . . .*

On warm days, you lay her naked on the ground on a soft blanket and wrap your bright scarves around her body and watch her laugh while you snap pictures for when you are not so sleep deprived and have time to remember. You take her to baby massage class, and learn to plant a garden on her back. First, you smooth her skin to get the soil all ready, and with small circular movements, you plant peas, string beans, corn, onions, kale, strawberries, and raspberries, covering all of them, and lightly watering them until they grow. (Now your kidney bean turned 16-year-old asks you to plant a garden on her back after two hours of volleyball practice, and you plant her favorite: lemon cucumbers, and basil, before she falls asleep in her 10x12 shed turned bedroom, aka the little house.)

You pump, you breastfeed, you massage your breasts when they are engorged or infected, you want to stop, but all the moms in the baby group say *no, no, keep going, the pain will subside* and it does finally, after 9 months of cracked nipples and crying when she latches on, and then you love it, lying in the bathtub with her floating off you and sucking away like some precious flotsam in the ocean swell. You nurse on and on, after most all of the other moms have stopped. *Mommy, it tastes like chocolate,* she says and she's too big to lie in your arms, but has to sit up to drink, even past the point when hardly any milk is coming out, except the comforting kind, the kind you want to go on forever because it is the body that binds you, the pulsing root to limb of this kidney bean-turned-baby-turned-toddler, who has started to memorize books and doesn't like to play in the mud and sits on the merry-go-round like the buddha and watches the world whir by, unfazed by the noise or people clapping. Mothers in the store ask if you've adopted her from China or Vietnam and you spit out *she came out of my own uterus, you asshole* (which you don't say but want to) and you wonder how love came to be an external attribute when all you want is to wrap your arms around her and keep her close, even as you hope she grows wings like a pelican, and soars into the sky, traveling through the fragile and enormous umbilical moments of the world.

# Source

Pines whisper your origins from moon
flavor too sweet for dreams. Face
round like cool orange skin, eyes
the color of fudge sundaes.
In the car you practice all the words you know:
*Mama, up, down, come, wait,*
*baby, nu nu, sleeping cat.*
We run like cats in the playground
a blur of calico tuft, feet hardly
touching the ground, swinging.
You lean your head backwards
to take in the upside down world,
yellowing leaves like sunlit fingers
smeared over the sky.
After the ride, arms canopied wide,
one leaf sticks in your collar, I say
the tree gave you a gift from her arms—
clutching it, you will take it home,
show your daddy what the earth offered
you, show your daddy what the earth has given him.
You run like a brook toward
the source of all creation, a foal
kicking up dust, legs
splayed, knocking
on dreams, innocence
screaming to be kept alive.
Nestled against undressed
breasts, suckling
like a baby, you lightly
cup your hand over
the other nipple,
not touching but almost,
the most tender move.

I want to make the world sing for you,
spread her branches wide. I want to
give you kisses behind the knees,
a poem or a day you can come home to.
Dance you into a frenzy, into an ocean
so sweet, lovers ache
to drink there.

# The Wall Between

We're sitting on a picnic table talking about God.
I am trying to make sense, known to unknown,
sparkle of dew on a blade of grass in the early morning sun,
that mysterious force called love that can build you up
or destroy you. Her foot slices the air back and forth,
small fingers brush stray wisps from her eyes,
then fiddle with the fingers of her poncho.

At seven, she's seen many pass through:
the spotted towhee that died as we pulled
into the Bird Rescue Center and buried in the oat grass
with a song; the goldfish, Orange Smoothie; great-grandma
Felisa, laid out in white at the front of the church; her friend
Pablo who had just turned four, who used to gaze at water
from the hose, listening for secrets no adult could decipher.

Catalpa leaves shiver in the breeze, their long
seed pods sharp as daggers. My daughter leans
against my chest, back brushing my stomach,
heart beating through the thin T-shirt, vibrating
against the edge of my ribs. *I know what God is, Mama.*
*God is the wall between life and death, a wall*
*that is easily broken, like porcelain.*

For a moment everything stops, the blue jays shrieking
in the maples, the wind, my breath. Strands of her hair
weave through the air, as if her form has shifted
into shadow I cannot place my hands on.
When I look again, I can almost see the blue clay
of her body, like a bowl, solid but smooth,
fragile as glass.

# Tethered

From a distance, she could have been anyone's,
polka-dotted dress, easy long stride,
a dusky, beveled pouring out that says
the world is mine, but for the shared DNA,
electric on my ribs, in my mouth.
Many years back, in her car seat,
I sensed her falling asleep, my breath
shifting to a slow-down to match hers,
this umbilicus, tight. Tethered to a spring heat,
apple blossoms white as clouds, the grip shimmies
close as she comes closer, rippling in and
out on a wave that knocks me out
and later when I'd pulled into your driveway
unbidden, the car driving itself, bypassing
the hour to give you a long-wished for hug,
the sound of the body there again—
keeper of the bones
propelled back to itself
being born.

# From the Shore

I could almost see the shape of her miles
off, as if my glasses were triple washed—
first azure, zinc, then the foreground of
oystercatchers digging for clams.
As if an invisible knife on the
diagonal, cutting the ocean
in half, could twist
these many years into
more wanting I can hardly touch.

She will start again, newly born and my
womb will insist not enough time
to go back, start again but the door
already opened, stands waiting.
I want to give her the frozen and the heat,
bodies that will love and leave her,
as if her own heart in its small shell
is a boat sailing off, all of us waving
from the shore, as she recedes
and emerges on the other side.
As if there is anything else.

# Day at Pinnacle Gulch

Shadows drown the sea
backlit as falling leaves,

lick the sandy shore, eroding
seconds into whitecaps.

Still, the hot beach
reaches back into

itself, a cascading rhythm,
a metronome of forward march.

When she walks in her yellow pants,
tight around the cheeks

small bodies hum

at our feet, scattered
in the salty breeze—

I the boat
you the oar—

together swells like
windswept dogs
roll over, again

and again and again.

# Growing Up

I.

Black hair down her back like
pale lichen hanging off oak and bay,
threading our way into redwoods,
fog beneath us, whipped cream hovering
above the steely water, boots on moist dark ground.
How will I ever wave good-bye?

II.

Measuring her torso with the pink measuring tape
that snaps back when you press the button,
we go through the list: gaiters, base layer, long underwear,
65-liter backpack. Her fingers at high speed
wrapping the blue wool around the needles,
the scarf lengthening as the light wanes.

III.

Forking the polenta, greens
and blueberry pancakes into my mouth, the waiter
speaking quick, she says, *I don't like asking you for money/
I don't want debt when I get to college,* shaky hands calmed from
the food sliding down my throat, her hands cutting
the avocado into small, equal slices.

IV.

They were supposed to make risotto but he changed his mind,
wanted to go to a movie she'd never heard of, so I made
lentil soup and salad, their laughter floating past
the Xmas tree, gliding into the air, his hair pulled back in a
ponytail, still nervous around me after two years. She said she was
too tired. We watched a movie that haunted me, even days later.


V.

I'm afraid to wear the pink socks she knitted me for my birthday.
Soft, like Neruda's rabbits, I want to frame them,
feed them sunshine and mint,
in the card was part of his poem
*what is good is doubly good . . .*
but the hole popped up, like a kiss, out of life's imperfections.


VI.

The secret: we still stick our tongues out when no one is looking.
I lie in bed, counting, one year and eight months before she flies
away. Fierceness rises up, her body in my body,
now another millennium, and the skin
sings with her heartbeat, tender between my ribs.

She is mine
        she is not mine
she is mine
        she is her own.

# Ode to the Tiny House

*House says*   I am an opaque shell of piano music played
late under the stars.
*House says*   I am where you fell asleep with your arms
around your child's shoulders and woke at midnight
to prepare the next day's lesson.
*House says*   from a tiny buddha to a 16-year-old
chef, painter, intellectual, she grew.
*House says*   I am the shelter for romance, re-kindled, first
a smoldering ash, a conflagration, then a blue, steady flame.
*House says*   under my eaves, dubbed the one-room schoolhouse,
you laughed till you peed, cried yourself to sleep, danced naked
and rose in shock at extremism.
*House says*   here is the sanctuary for tending aging parents, those
insomniac nights, worried financial days, emergency calls at 2am.
*House says*   inside my walls you are a poem, a gourmet meal,
a woman cross-legged on a pillow, four middle-schoolers talking at
once in the kitchen.
*House says*   when you leave I will remain, holding these windows
open for the moments to flutter out, whisper, then settle inside.

## Soprano of Our Singing


You are flowing liquid in my cells
circulating in these small rooms
a strummed guitar     soprano of our singing.
In these fascia, dinosaurs roam     laughter
at their bigness threaded with crisscrossed roots.
You are creative spirit pulsing the moment alive
    adventurer in traveling feet
        DNA of my bone marrow
a quiet goodbye slipping down a mother's cheeks.
Independent, wise like the current,
kind, compassionate as a doe in the meadow,
    loyal friend, cousin for the whole of it
        a community parade, the best meal ever.
Joy, windswept, illuminating those you touch—
you are mountain vistas, glittering forests,
hot air balloon and hard-packed earth,
running to inhale,
extract every ounce
from this scissored beauty—

your destiny calling, dancing you home,
dancing you to your truest desires.

# IV.

## Future On A Pillow

# The New Season

In spring, carbon in the air dips
her magenta blossoms like
a faun's tender lips. Thick
white fists petal the sidewalk,
and bees dusted with sunlight
drink themselves drunk on the
fragrance. How can pink
apple petals hold the risk
of a no future future?

If only we would
listen to the coral,
to the language of fire
and the crack of melting
glaciers.

Every note ever sung lives in them.

Yet somehow we still trust that in autumn, light
will echo off crisp long days
the apple tree will lose her leaves
as a woman drops eggs, and earthworms
will eat up our soil
while carbon
continues to rise
and naysayers fall from their pulpits,
redwoods working overtime to eat up this invisible
gas trapped like greed's last meal.

Some say nothing is the place we all began
and to where we shall return

some say this is the new earth breathing.

# Tubbs Fire, 2017

That other fire started from a love letter
written by an irate forest ranger
whose passion got the best of her
in a Colorado campground as woodpeckers dug
for worms, a hawk crying above scattered stars.

This first time might have been a kiss from the earth
a wake-up call, to evacuate our ways
out of those metal boxes heating us up
if only we don't hang
up, pretend it's an aberration, if only
we'd sit up and listen to the clamor.

This is our battle, racing from smoke and flames,
waking at three a.m. to check
evacuation updates, no power, no water,
elders on stretchers, glued to the radio, shelters overflowing.
Language of disaster, a vocabulary that never used
to fit in our mouths, now rolling out fluently,
ubiquitous, as if we cannot remember
how to breathe in calm.

At the shelter, trucks with supplies, stop,
unload: shoes, sun hats,
diapers, shampoo, underwear, soap.
I box them up, bring them in, go back for more.
Kindness opens my lungs, smoke closes
them down. *Grief and love, excitement and fear*

*live in the same part of the brain,* they say.
The only salve for burning is to keep moving, self
to self, sink to desk, back to phone, aimless wandering,
unfamiliar country, cracking open with each tiny step.

## What If

Cherry tomatoes cling to the vine, contrasting
the ashy light, un-ready to leap
into the bowl. Liminal days of yellowish
smoke, packing and repacking the go-bag,
weighing what to keep, what to leave behind.

I remember as a child standing beside the phone
while the flames engulfed the room, mesmerized
by its shape, the way it knew no bounds,
could eat up air, swallow us whole
in one hungry, wordless blow.

After it had its way we surveyed
the carcass of the house, the day
impossibly alive where the walls
should have been, tiny mimosa
seedling I had potted the week before
and the tears that would not fall, like rain.

What if the tilt toward emptiness, not the boundless
spread of stars or the mountain top's breadth,
could open the gates of the heart?

What if the beating of our pulse
sifting time with an owl's patience,
could be enough?

What if the soft tomato
taste of summer, the blue skin
of love like the flutter of swallows
in the sky were ours?

Who would we be then?

## Months Later, What Remains

Under the hood, fine powdery ash
on my fingers, the air on Mark West Springs
bitter beneath the tongue,
tightens my jaw like gunshot.
How to show you the rounded shoulders,
a slower gait, dark patches under the eyes
of those who lost every finite thing?
This city I married when the alveoli
could not take in any more love, is someone else now.
Tender green shoots sprout on charred
hillsides, homeowners spread blueprints,
lawsuits await briefs, but her breath, there at the quiet
spot at the end of the exhale, catches for a second,
and her face, ever so slightly hidden, is weary
at the edge of that smile.

# Camp Fire

Thick-throated, eyes
like small sticks, water-logged

ache in the lungs. Trees so still
it almost looks like snow

in New York in December.
Heart doesn't want to inhale

this dialect stirred up
on the deserted street

listening between the lines.

A daughter's picture
from fifth grade, the

beaded necklace she made
with the turquoise clasp, her

favorite songbook, the one
with the parrot in the margins.

I walk the empty sidewalks,
breathing in so many lives.

Like frosted glass in a car, long ago
turned off, the memory idles:

blackened trees, rivers of ash,
birdsong in some
other paradise.

# In the DMV

to renew my license, her story
sifts into me, a fine powdered

snow. M.'s husband died (only 59) two months before
the Tubbs Fire, the first year of the rest of our lives. She

moved to Mark West Springs Road the day before
the flames ate it all up, sped out with the aid

of a stranger she's never found. Tears
shine her cheeks as she shuffles my documents

in a pile. People wait behind me on hard, gray plastic
chairs. *G134* rings over the PA system, here and there

people at computers take the permit test.
My burning hand stretches to touch

hers. The place we lay our heads,
burrow into, the future on a pillow

gone before she could wipe the ring from the tub.

*Cray cray* she says. *I used to be a manager at Kaiser,
16-hour days, but here I am among friends.*

*After work, the quiet of leaves, that painted sky under
my feet just takes me away for miles.*

# V.

# Build Me a Mountain

# New Year's 2020, B.C. (Before Covid)

Hopeful decade, discordant
abandon. All things wither to be set

free. Old lovers hold hands vowing not to
leave the other. Still, one door opens

while the other stays shut, even if we
do not want the sparrows to sing.

Remember when next year was the future,
shiny like a found penny on the sidewalk?

A vow for the rest of our lives:
to laugh more, to make art, to love like

there's no lifeline where we are headed
except our own resilient natures,

greedy, kind, giving with one hand, taking
with the other. Believe in tilting

the face toward beauty, the urge
to give up a seat to those who cannot

stand, believe in adaptation, deep as
evolutionary microbes, eating us

from the outside in, and change,
that sly beast, always the only

hook we can hang our coats on.

# Exile

In a land where no one speaks
the same language, the body
becomes an island

a solitary refuge
we escape into, a soft
nest of leaves and debris
we can wrap around us and say

*touch me with your fragile lips*
*build me a mountain*
*let me wake up tomorrow*
*greater than I am today.*

# End of Days

Shimmering weight on the head,
sweat streaming down torso,
dark houses, power and people
cloistered, scattered in masked
lethargy, desperate for elections to ease
the trembling. Early morning palpitations,
dry grass, iron stillness (when did fire
become a season), another lurking
fast and furious in the moments
between sleep, fearing gusts of wind
in the eucalyptus (when did autumn
sound like dread). One day you went

to the beach for a hit of hope
and the red tide shot up your nose
acrid, metallic, like when you haven't cried
in a long time and it all comes pouring out.
You say *show me what isn't coming undone*
walking on the bones of the dead
whispering to their invisible eardrums
you say *might as well carve memory into air*
like cupping unfettered desires,
their rotten stink in the teeth
of your hands.

# Escape

We head to the coast in a world
that seems so benign: chartreuse hillsides
dotted with grazing cows, turkey vultures
soaring on the updraft, where the act of driving
away from confinement, like outlaws
on the run, makes us giddy with freedom.
There, the Pacific, in her infinite blueness
caresses the empty spots with her shine,
the way a mother soothes the forehead
of a sick child. Even from the required
distance, the crest of her body lulls us
in the sunshine, feet dangle from the open
tailgate and we drink her in after a long dry spell,
thirsty for her expansive reach, for some kind of
possibility outside the same four walls of bad
news and masks, just a long view
of the horizon, where we might drown ourselves
in her sapphire arms and come through
a doorway, right out the other side.

# What Was Once a Street

now a river, a lake, creates
its own language, knows
no fences except to fall in love
with gravity, slithering
under oaks, between
sidewalks, nowhere to go except
forward, a bottomless pool
that could engulf you if you let it,
that would carry you away in your metal box
into the next day or hour or maybe into yesterday,
while the mustard flowers sprout
up in February, golden-tinged as a rusty fender.
You don't succumb to inertia. You plow into the sea
wanting to overturn your slipping
heart, you pray to become
a boat on the waves. Inch by inch
the pond you swim through parts
like that other story. The bones
of dinosaurs under your body
reminds you the earth is a mountain,
a ladder of stars glued to
birth, lament. The car hits cement,
your pulse a rebirth, intangible
as a red-tailed hawk
wheeling under the translucent sky.

## After Lockdown

In this baby state, thick cushion of sand
goes on for miles and miles, children laugh amid

waves, oystercatchers pick at the shore
with curved beaks, only to put it back

whole. Families build cities
out of glass, dogs dig for clams,

rhythmic lull of tides between
my soul sister and me: her for sky, me for earth.

After eating only fear, the small
world of walls, masks,

*don't touch that*
the taste of a burger and fries

quenches some deep abiding empty.
Tiny, inexplicable cracks overflow—

*I am alive*
*I am joy, dance me*

cool water
blue mist

—we are let loose to swim anywhere
our arms can take us.

# Back to the Wild

In ferns and flowering oxalis beneath grandmother
redwoods, I find the self unafraid of society
breaking into unmanageable shards.
Nettles and wild iris, purple as
a bruise, sway in the breeze, singing
in ancient tongues. Gracie says
*I could live in the woods,* happy and unencumbered,
as we walk over bay and oak roots and miles
of mycelium, a parachute threaded with our
shared genetic bones. Sitting on redwood duff,
sunlight reflects a perfect circular
web, and I am unwilling to walk back,
wanting to halt time, like the red-shouldered
hawk soaring above us

to become a new kind of stillness,
a new kind of alive.

## Ode to Resilience

Ball that falls but bounces
back up, clean blue-kissed sky
after fires sweep through.

The feel of her pressed into the curve
of my back, spooning me
like an empty bowl. Laughing

at one thing then another
even though we know
we are going straight to—

Exhaustion that pins arms to bed
followed by tomorrow's skip,
the way rubber bands snap back.

Mulchy rain smell after months of
drought, some terrible reason to weep
then the poem that heals. Kind glance

from a lonely day stranger.
Flooded rooms where the tiniest
earthworm, alive, floats by, no

running water then a friend's
arms around my shoulders.

Violin melody and love
out a window just for me.

# VI.

## If Not for His Hands

# The Life You Gave Me

*for my grandfather*


It could not fit in a velvet box with a
velour ribbon tied twice nor could it be worn,
an evening gown blue as the generous, sad sea.
Not a stone, not a car, not a dog with pleading
eyes to please get the bone before it's gone forever.
It wasn't green, it didn't sing but started quiet
as an egg splitting in the waters. Not chapped hands
in winter, not webs behind the bed, not the pitch
perfect way oaks whip in a storm.
Listen to this gift burn. Air coming and going
in a nostril. Upper eyelid drooped and creased,
a delicate gate. The way I open the door with my left,
close it with my right. Footfall on tile. You watching me
in my dreams, reaching your eyes out as if to say
*take it, I don't need it where I'm going*
arms laden with white roses, one for each year
you lost, one for each of mine.

# Great Blue Heron

Jogging the track in early morning hush, trucks in the distance
ripping up concrete, I remember my grandmother, how she told

of standing in the New York subway, two small sets of hands in
her own, how she wanted to throw herself onto the tracks, but their

faces peered up at her, those sad, empty mouths, and this stopped
her. I wonder now how she made it through, how she forced

herself to turn on the tap, scraping last night's dishes. How she
sewed and sewed until her skin cracked. A great blue heron

wings into the center of the wet field, its body an
exclamation point, neck like a pencil, turned toward the east.

Its elegance unmoors me and I turn back every few
seconds to watch it glide without touching ground, like the stone

statue game I used to play in the woods by the creek.
The heron elongates, plumage a steely gray touched by the sky.

How do we keep from throwing it away? How do we stand
still and listen? Blue heron jabs her beak into the moist grass,

throws back her serpentine neck, oblivious to my presence. She
could be the center of everything, all of us rotating in concentric

orbits, spinning with the shifting light, flailing our arms in a dance
of form and shadow. Now the heron hears a noise, opens her

wings, lifts the sun over my head. My feet dig
into the soil, my voice in that other lifetime, so quiet,

begging to be released.

# Saying No to Treatment

The palliative care nurse
never once says the word, like
a rhinoceros dangling from the
center of the table. Tomorrow
exhales below the skin
but she is kind, she will come
back, we are not

alone. My mother, after a lifetime
of shoveling pills into her body, gives it away
for the scariest ride, vertical
descent, mouth open, arms
up, free fall through the

raucous void.

Sign documents, open and sort the mail,
pen more forms, make phone calls, fill the
lockbox, write the rent check, pay the caregiver,
give the cat her pain meds.

Her hand trembles in her lap. The pianist, Simone
Dinnerstein, makes love to the Steinway,
Bach and Mozart pour like
cream from a silver pitcher.
My mother's lips murmur to the
flurry of melody on

wind-swept keys.

Money dwindles away. I have to shout
it alive. Each year floats into the sea.
I don't know about winter
except my mother's once tall frame

now hunched over white-socked
feet, and crippled hands
pulling herself along to the wheeled
hum of the walker. This window, this
silhouette. The fire in her breath
caught at the inhale.

# Apple Valley Skilled Nursing

*for my stepfather*

A flock of egrets
shimmering white—
his cold, dry hand

against mine. Urine and bleach
in the nose, frayed red carpet, folded up
wheelchair. *I'm so lonely here.*
His eyes and his voice, a droplet,

a train pulling into
a station, my mother's hands,
gnarled, like winter.

Apple tree, yellow leaves,
wet ground. After
phone calls, emails, bills,
still I feel I have failed him.

Rotation toward shortest light,
elongated shadows.
I thought he'd go quickly.
Now he's caught between

black hat on his head,
old skin on his body,
TV blaring, and his
roommate yelling his wife's name.

One moment he says his apartment
has disappeared, the next
he is a young man in shorts
riding a bike in morning

sunshine. Dusky sky smudged
with stars, rattle of walker, now
the cat on my mother's lap, his chair
full of papers, skeins of yarn.

His son sends an email—
*contact me when he dies.*
The aide fluffs up his pillows,
smiles at him before turning to go.
The next moment my stepdad is the same
guy I remember, thanking
me for coming.
He says *I hope I don't outlive my money.*

# Don't Turn the Light On

My mother bends down and whispers into Jarvis's ear, *don't turn the light on,* hoping he'll fail so he'll come back. Jarvis is a yellow Labrador with dark brown eyes, soulful as a well, with a bit of deeper orange around his muzzle. His fate is to be a service dog if doggie college goes well, and my mother is saying good-bye to him after a year and a half of him mostly lying on the carpet with his pointy nose resting on his paws, like an old dog set out to pasture.

I take my mom to the doctor, and her large breasts swing heavily under her salmon-colored tee-shirt, white hair sticking up in tiny tendrils around her ears. She rises from her chair, head almost to the floor, back bent, so slowly I think her feet aren't going to make contact with the carpet and clutches the walker to get herself to the bathroom.

A few years ago my stepdad, Don, called me, anxiety punctuating his speech, because he sent off a check, but couldn't remember who he'd sent it to. Last year I was woken up at 1am by a nurse because my mother took too much morphine, panicked and called 911. The nurse told me they wouldn't keep her, and if I didn't get her, they would throw her in a cab. My mother has called me screaming when my stepfather hit her because she turned the heat down, and when I met the police there, they asked him what month it was and who the president was. Last week I got a call from a strange cell number telling me they were stranded in the parking lot of the podiatrist, waiting for para-transit that never came. When I showed up, all the offices were closed, the parking lot empty, and there were my parents sitting on their walkers, looking terribly vulnerable.

A friend who'd been taking care of her aging parents told me she'd consulted a rabbi once. According to this rabbi, the Talmud states that a child should not sacrifice too much for their parents. Somehow that makes me feel better when I fantasize about running away to (insert country with beautiful remote beaches) and never coming back. Trying to protect their tiny savings account from drying up before they die exhausts me. There have been days when I turned off my phone and instructed them to call 911 for the next emergency, or not been present for medical appointments, so that they promptly forgot everything the doctor said. I stayed in bed when at midnight my mother called in a panic from her bedroom floor, unable to get up, and yelled at me that I was a bad daughter for leaving her there (I couldn't have picked her up anyway—she was 175 lbs.). I have lied a dozen times that I have a headache and couldn't come over, when I just couldn't face making one more grilled cheese sandwich and seeing them so old, so cranky, so needy. When I just couldn't stand watching one more Ingrid Bergman re-run with my mother's bony hand in mine.

Mostly over the last several years, I've wanted them to die, depending on how trapped I've felt. Not REALLY die, but just not need me so desperately, so that I could just go over, sit in their maroon chairs, and talk about the absurdity of politics. Just have them pet Jarvis, and leave with the satisfying click of the metal gates behind me, knowing I wasn't needed in any life or death way.

But my mom is a Holocaust survivor. All my life I have felt as if I needed to protect her from suffering. From the loneliness and heartache of being alive. My mother makes me laugh. Her eyes look at me with so much admiration. My heart finds hers when we sit next to each other and she sighs, content to have me near. She birthed me. She knows me. We are inextricably bound by fierce love and grief.

Yesterday my mom asked me if the symptoms don't come back, does that mean the cancer went away. I said that eventually the cancer will spread and her body will start to change. She said, *but if I have surgery I might never get out of bed*. From a woman who for thirty years reached for a plethora of pills to fix her aches and pains, I am proud that she's refusing surgery, even if it might buy her more time.

Don doesn't usually say much anymore, but last week he came up to give me a hug, and said, "How do you like my new glasses? Don't they make me look smart?" I am lucky because my parents are essentially still there, even if they get confused and can't remember what day it is. They are shorter, wrinkled, in pain, wobbly, angry at times, and sometimes grateful, but they still read the paper daily, concerned about the state of this country and concerned about me. So in the meantime, I do what a dutiful daughter should. I pay the bills, fill the morphine lockbox, pencil in the appointments, bring them quarters for laundry, and talk to doctors. Because one day there will be no one to make sandwiches for, and no dog to usher across their threshold and no fumbling with the remote and listening to my mother swear at the TV when she wants to watch yet another Bergman re-run in the brown recliner with the heat turned up to 90.

## The Beast

Soft flesh and brittle bones mark my stepfather's spot
on the leather chair, the indentation his fork leaves on the table.
Memory runs through him, a skittish cat racing from a stranger,
what he ate for breakfast replaced by the name of his
best friend in the Second World War.
So many grooves to retrieve over a lifetime.

Then anger resettles his face. In my periphery, I catch a glint
in his eyes, some bit of fur. Trapped and pacing in his small
cage, he walks back and forth as if this could free him.

His mind belongs to you or me or
the woman ranting in front of the bank,
talking in the voices of crows.

The doctor is afraid of him. I have seen it.
I am afraid of him. I have seen that too.

The beast paces, the one with yellow eyes and fangs
ready to claw me into submission and swallow me. Bit by bit,
I turn into that maniacal president, the homophobic skinhead.
When I jump up, slam my hand down and scream,
a tiger leaps over bars into another kind of chaos, my heart
throbbing, cacophony bright as the sun.

Freedom owes nothing to silence, everything to action.
He backs away, lowers himself into human form.
For a long time, my body quivers like a house in a violent gale,
shifting on its foundation, trying to find the joists that will keep
it upright and steady.

I sit at the window, let the light find me,
planning my escape.
When I hear my voice again,
only a hint of a growl just below the surface,
the sound comes from anywhere but my mouth.

# VII.

# You Won't Forget Me

# Mishegas

I don't need anyone else.
B. shops, mops, does the laundry.
We can take the shuttle to the podiatrist.
If someone comes, they have to be over 40. I don't want
anyone too young. What if they want my jewelry?
Remember that girl with the jalopy?
I don't want to drive around in a car
I don't know. It might smell bad.

You lost how much money a month? How could you
give up your class? Oh, that was because of his
stroke. See, it's all my husband's fault.
Oh, my God, that's a lot of money. Well, I know
you can't just say give it back but
it was yours in the beginning and they should
know that. Can you maybe say it was a mistake?

You don't need to come two times a week. I'd love
to see you but we can manage without your
help. All we do is watch TV, eat some cottage cheese
with peaches, read a little, fall asleep.
You keep telling me you're tired
so rest a little, don't keep running around.

Oh, by the way, I need to go to the eye
doctor. Can you make an appointment and
take me? Also, the vacuum cleaner finally
is kaput. I'd like you to drive me to Sears so
I can buy another one. Then I want you to pick
up the mail. When I get my pension, you
can deposit it, and then write our rent check.

You really ought to get more sleep. You've got those
dark circles under your eyes, and you're putting on
weight. A mother sees everything.
You should get a job that pays
better. Like Diane's son.
He's in construction.

# Look Harder

I have a story for you.

I made P. a poncho for $40. She told me she'd given
it to a friend, she never wore it. Then she asked if I'd like
to have it back. And I said I'd return
the money she paid me.

Isn't that stupid? Well, I'm mad at myself. I shouldn't
have given her the money back. She could have just returned
the poncho and I'd have the $40 too.

We are $500 short on our rent this month?
I really can't afford to be so generous
with my ponchos. Have you tried the Austrian pension
people again? Still no check? Every day I'm waiting
and every day you tell me it hasn't come.
I really hate living like this.

I remember when I was a kid and Mom couldn't afford
to give me five cents for an ice cream cone, so I did without,
while all the other kids on the block ran out to the truck.
Humiliating.

Well, I hope you can find those slippers. I've been walking around
in my socks for the last year, it hurts the corn on the bottom
of my foot. I know that corn is gone, but I just want
something softer I can wear in the house. The doctor
even thought it was a good idea.

These shoes fit really well—-they're perfect. After the eighth pair
they should be. $103? You can take the money out
of the savings account. There's plenty of money
in there. Don't worry so much. You should try
some of my morphine. When I take it everything looks rosier.

I was talking to J. the other day. She told me she pays $200
in rent and the government pays for everything else.
That will happen to me when he dies. When I run out of money,
I'll get free slippers, shoes and food.
Oh, it doesn't work like that?
I make too much every month?
Well, if we make too much, how come we can't pay our rent?

It's the curse of the middle class. What, they think we're sitting
around in a mansion with servants at our beck and call? Don needs
a new bridge. That will cost $1,000 and his mattress
has a hole in it. I think it's about 30 years old.

I feel bad I never gave you a Christmas present.
I'll give you a check for $100. No?
Look harder, I'm sure it's there.

# Morphine Hell

*My mother started with Demerol in the late 1970s for pain associated with menopause. From there it was a slippery slope to oxycontin and then morphine. At 66, my mother was admitted to a lockdown facility to withdraw cold turkey because doctors would no longer prescribe her medications. That night, delirious from pain, she fell and broke her back, which landed her in the hospital, back on morphine. At 81 years old, my mother often took too many pills to stem the pain and at some point, the pain clinic doctor refused to refill her supply, even though her symptoms were akin to a heroin withdrawal. Once, in an attempt to stave off the pain, she reached for her husband's medications and ended up in the emergency room. This last scenario inspired this writing.*

Claire, I'm at the hospital. My body just didn't feel right. I was really hot, and my legs wouldn't work. I couldn't sleep so I took one of Don's pills, the tiny red one, the one that makes him sleep. Oh, it's not a sleeping pill? It's antipsychotic? Well, it just made my legs move all over the place and my body was on fire. That's when I called 911. That ambulance was so cold. I don't know why they can't heat it for their patients. Can you come get me? I know it's late, but I thought you'd be here by now. I took my last pill today and then I had a terrible fight with Don. I wanted my cereal and he said I couldn't have it, so he hid it and I couldn't get to it. I started yelling and screaming, I was so mad. I had acupuncture earlier, and he ruined all of it. I want him to just go away. Yeah, put him in a nursing home. He called me a fat pig. Nice, isn't it? To be married to someone all these years, and that's what they say to you? He doesn't care about me. Yeah, dementia, whatever—he's always been like that. I don't know how I was so short on pills. You know that new girl who started last week? I think it's her. Well, maybe I did take a few extra but the pain in my feet was so bad I couldn't stand it. I need some pain medicine now. Can you come and tell them to give it to me?

I'm so glad you came. Can you help me to the bathroom? They said I fell asleep? I never went to sleep, they're making that up. My legs are so restless, it's awful. I can barely stand up. I just came in my nightgown—I forgot to take a robe. Oh, look at the moon out the hospital window. It's so nice, I never get to see it from my bedroom. Did I tell you about my neighbor? She's going downhill fast, she can't really leave her apartment anymore. A car accident when she was 16 left her paralyzed. So sad. Did they give me something for anxiety?

Claire, thank God you're here. I can't get out of bed. At least it's my own bed, and I'm not stuck in a hospital hallway. I just want to slit my wrists. I need you to fill the prescription. But why can't they fill it? You have the piece of paper. The pain in my stomach is so bad and I have a terrible headache. What did you bring me? Will it make me sleepy? What about these little white pills? Homeo what? I know you've had good luck with that. I need you to go to the pain clinic, and then the pharmacy. The diarrhea will start soon. It always does. Get me some Imodium. You have not seen me like this 20 times, maybe only a few times. I have to get rid of this pain. Just tell them your mother's senile, and she couldn't tell which pills were which, tell them I'm throwing up. You know, really tell them a story. The doctor won't OK it because it's not life and death? But you have the prescription!! And it is life and death. I feel like killing myself. Get me the lock box. I can't go through this again. I know I yelled at you last time, but I can't do this anymore. That stupid doctor. He didn't even have the courage to call you and tell you himself. Nice. What a bunch of bastards. I'm an old lady. How can they treat an old lady like this?

# Like A Miracle

I think my mind is going sideways.
Today I was dizzy; I could barely stand it.
But now I have a story. Listen to this.

You know our vacuum broke, and we borrowed B.'s vacuum. We've had it for a long time, and she said we could keep it, she doesn't need it, but I feel funny. What if she wanted it back? Anyway, she took our broken vacuum to the vacuum repair guy and he said he needed to order a part for it, but when she checked back with him, he kept saying he couldn't get the part.

B. is really something. So she told him that she was picking it up even though it wasn't fixed, and taking it to another guy.

This new guy said that he could fix it without the part and it would cost less than a hundred dollars. That could mean $99, but whatever. So I hung up and told B. I would talk it over with Don. But his mind is going sideways too. He keeps talking about calling the Austrian Consulate about my pension, and I keep telling him they have nothing to do with it, but he doesn't listen.

So when he and I were talking about the vacuum, B. called back and said the vacuum was fixed! Like a miracle!

He had fixed it without even ordering the new part, while we were trying to figure out what to do. I think the other guy must have been confused, maybe his mind was going sideways too. Maybe he was just stringing us along, maybe he didn't know what he was doing. He's been in business 30 years, you'd think he would know how to fix a lousy vacuum. We could have kept B.'s vacuum, but I wouldn't have felt right about it. She is so nice to us, she really goes above and beyond, calling this guy and schlepping it back and forth.

And what about my pension?

I can't stand it anymore. Just call them, will you, and take it out of our account. It needs to be done, once and for all. It's been dragging on and I feel like a pauper when you tell me I can't spend money. And what about Don's doctor. You told me he doesn't have one and he says he won't go back to that doctor with the same last name as us, what was it? Oh, Williams. He says that she didn't even touch the stethoscope to his body, which I don't really understand. You told her how he tried to hit me? Oh, right, he actually did hit me. I forgot. Anyway, you need to get him another doctor as soon as you can, even if he doesn't need one. What if he keels over tomorrow from an aneurysm?

You know your Omi had an aneurysm that she discovered because her eyes kept burning. Those burning eyes saved her life. Your grandmother was really something and already 85. In the hospital, when they come in to check if your mind is sideways, and ask you what day it is, and who the president of the United States is, do you know what she said? *Why don't you ask me something really hard, like who the prime minister of Israel is?*

One more thing.

You always have to get back to work, no time for your old mother. If you didn't run around so much, then you wouldn't get sick, and you could spend more time with me. You told me the puppy got an infection. The worry kept me up all night. It should be brought to the vet right away. They can't wait until tomorrow. It could die. I know it's not your dog, but you can tell this guy he should listen to your mother. I raised both of you, took care of you when you were sick. I know a thing or two. You can tell him that a sick dog isn't a good sign. You don't want it going backwards.

# Release Me

Now that it's started,
I don't think you'll be able to go to Italy.
It was everywhere: on the floor, my clothes,
at least it didn't get on the chair.

I won't have to go to the nursing home now.
You can cancel all of the appointments.
I won't need that man. What was his name?
The tall one missing the finger.
He was very nice.

Can you get me some V8 juice?
And don't screw the lid down too tight after you pour it.
I should have died a long time ago.
I'm a burden. Terrible. But it's not my fault.
I was in terrific pain and I needed a pill.

Was it thirty years ago I started?
Now those little purple pills are my lifeline.
I dropped one the other day and oy vey, did I scream!
I will miss that nice doctor. I liked his hands on my knee.

I didn't have a father, and my mother worked all the time to
support us. I'm sorry your father was not a good dad.
I just didn't know a good one from a nebbish.

I'll die soon enough and you can go back to your poetry.
What would you rather do, anyway?
Spend time with your mother or write a silly poem?

You won't forget me after I go, I'll tell you that.
You won't forget me.

# VIII.

# The Leaving Place

# Mushrooming at Salt Point

Foraging in damp forest, dripping with jade hues
I listen to stillness, to forget the dying time.

No plague, no lonely, no lost mother among
tan oaks and witches butter yellow as cream.

Only the sweet talk of friends, the exhilaration
when a purple hedgehog edges into view

above rain-drenched leaves, miles and miles
of underground byways, fecund as dreams

beneath our soles. Candy caps, russulas with crimson
faces, dark-shaped nipples like a woman on a motorcycle,

each mushroom a treasure, given when
we ask for nothing, when we turn lizard on

a clear afternoon, blood pooling, waiting
for the cool earthy smell to rinse us clean

of knowing, our fingertips on yellow gills,
creamy stipes, their small bodies prone

in our baskets like fairies, blending
into the verdant mulch, our minds

quiet, bent low, murmuring a language
we still don't understand:

matsutake, agaricus, chanterelle.

# The Promise

*after Audre Lorde's "Memorial"*

I was 11 when my mother said
*how could he do that to his father, how could
he abandon him?* Trees scraped

their fingers against a frosty window,
heard me promise, *I will never leave you, Mommy,*
her palm on my arm, fragile as a cobweb
moist with morning.

Lightly at first I combed her hair, nestled
in bed beside her, some longing needed me close
like dew on lilac before the world was born. I
gladly gave her my child-like laugh, having
no sounds for what the Nazis stole, the
beating of her pulse a rhythm of
not forgetting.

Later, I took the oath seriously. Middle of the night
emergency calls, yelling at the doctor
to feed her addiction, my mother's cries
ragged, bleeding me awake to an orange dawn.
Dead, I dreamed waking and sleeping. Not as
in forever dead but walking away, the promise
of ashes, a sliver of blue on my shoulder.

I fingered the pact like a survivor's river
rock in my pocket, dense with doing: click of the
morphine lock box I could fill blind, her desperate
pleas for companionship, sweets, old movies,
me sliding the Depends over
her swollen feet, tears hardened
stones inside my throat.

Silent and clear the sky after the last call.
The owl's dun-colored wings
separating night from day.

After, in a dream, my mother so
alive in a polka-dotted dress, red
and white tulips swaying in the
background for miles.

*Now you can lead your life,* she said
coming around the table
to hug me and I heard
the molten hiss of it dissolve
fiery, tender, like her whisper in my ear—

*I will always be here*
*I will never leave you.*

# Third Day of Hanukkah

On the third day, my
sister stuffs red pill after red pill
into my mother's cheeks to quell
her screams, the hospice

nurse at midnight, whose
parents were Viennese Jews
on the Kindertransport, feeds her
compassion and mercy from his own
hands. She is far away

when I arrive, slumped
in her recliner, head lolling, mouth
slack, a dedication to the makeshift
menorah, beeswax on a kitchen
plate, woven from the thick air of the room.

To witness the suffering of the outcasts.
To light a wick as if to say *I am yours alone,*
just enough in the covenant for a day.

I follow her shallow breaths, call my dear one,
the nurse, who says listen to the in and out
of her life, and I don't know where to start
counting, everything depends on the magic
number/six might be twice a third, as in the
beginning there was water and earth and
the scraping to let it be plenty and good.

To ease the pain of the treasured ones, the
desecrated time. To strike a match like a pulse,
just a drop of oil for this hour.

My heart gets in on it, makes up for the silence
between pauses. I gulp deeply as if I can keep
her on desire alone, as if the will of the
people, crying through the millennium, could
enter her body and pull her rooted to this spot

when the unbelievable happens, eight days of light
in her tiny apartment, my mother opens her eyes,
says hello in a small voice, eats a persimmon, drinks
some water, the fire elongates, wax
engraved like stone, like singing, she is

not going to die today
the tip of her heart and lungs still swelling,
she is in her chair, eating an orange fruit,
a gift, a miracle
from the blue and white
plate of the world.

## The Dying Time

In the hospital bed, an
operatic tune shoots from your

mouth, a trilling vibration, as if the ululating
cries carry you closer to the ethereal

edge, weight of your body
disappearing into refrain, into a tighter shell.

You could have been an opera singer except
a housewife, children, and career

were not woven into the 1950s,
so the music slipped away, those last years

almost nothing melodic except commercials
and old movie tracks on TV.

Above your head, a G, an A, a high B
undulate the air. You are running the scales,
betting on the sweet spot, humming
to be released.

We encircle you, sing you a
bridge, a language for your crossing

*lay yourself down on the rocks now*

three generations of women, chanting,
cradling you with our voices

*let your body down in the river*

sacred minutes, as if water empties you of song,
of sorrow buried deep in the cells

*listen to the drumming on the other side*

an invisible raft, lip of the horizon
you are destined for

*lose yourself in the meantime*

the leaving place,
where the call of blackbirds
with their red-tipped wings
can take your breath away.

# The Sound of You

I.  Every door I try to open
    disappears when I grasp the knob.
    No exit from this stab in the
    circle beneath the ribs,
    a flaming empty where
    your eyes used to be.

II. Morning and night the *phowa*
    practice, a clean sheet of light
    from the sound of you to somewhere bigger.
    Limbo, from the Latin
    *an edge or border*
    the smell of death stuck to the
    corners of your apartment
    like a lover who won't let go.

III. On your altar a blue skein of wool,
    bamboo needles, your favorite gold watch,
    a piece of Godiva chocolate, a photo of you
    with your mouth in mid-chew,
    the silk scarf, magenta and teal,
    the colors you loved and gave away,
    a square of wood etched with courage,
    a shell I kept in the shape of a heart.

IV. On my back in the pool
    melting into the sea above,
    a marble on the surface
    refracting sunlight,
    I am a body succumbing to
    weightlessness, you
    are the sky—
    everywhere I turn,
    slipping between my fingers.

# Disorientation

The Xmas tree rots, its smell fecund with decay. The corners of her apartment smell like death, where she lay overnight in the hospital bed in the living room, her spirit far away, her skin blue and cold. No wonder we lost our appetite. The kitchen table mere feet from her exit.

Decline, over years, slow as the sloth in the tree. But the last few weeks, swift like a river overflowing its banks, the water that swept her up in its claws and dropped her on the other side.

It started with a stroke and a year of recovery. Then her crippled feet and swollen knee, three times bigger than normal. After the uterine cancer diagnosis, months and months of back and forth with doctors, with each other, conversations like "to hysterectomy" or "not to hysterectomy." "Not to" won out but not after tug of war, tussles of will on all sides of the aisle. Many instances of Mom blaming us for the decision to keep her womb intact. Even the week before the lying down at the end, she looked me in the eye and said, "I think I will have to have that operation now." Always the quick fix, except surgery scared her, the unknown a bed she could not climb out of.

Two and a half years of no cancer symptoms, then bleeding, anxiety, panic. Was it the Chaga tincture or the slow-growing tumor? This last year her appetite lessened and her mind turned soft, like a sponge left too long in the sink. She could hear us, but not understand the sequence of the words, except the simple question, the simple answer. Those last months, incontinent, she walked around the apartment first in her underwear, then in her Depends. The circle closing, the snake eating its own tail.

Still, miraculously, in the middle of the night, alone, she would pull herself up out of the chair, onto the walker, and shuffle to the bathroom. The body's habit, cemented into the cells. I used to say she was weak in the will department, but it was there, in the hush when the world was asleep, keeping on keeping on.

Three years she lay in her recliner: morning, noon and night.

She made me buy two magnifying glasses. She said the newspaper print kept getting smaller. She could not understand what she read, but she followed Trump's antics like a sportscaster and lived to see him overthrown. Those last three months: hours of Olivia de Havilland movies, sleeping, eating eclairs and reading the daily circus of unraveling democracy.

I thought she'd never really die, even on the last day. She lived two weeks with no food and water. I didn't think that was humanly possible. That fear of the unknown. The morphine state at least familiar.

Now the emptiness, the quiet phone unmoor me.

She needed me for a decade. Now she doesn't need me for anything. Disoriented, I try to catch my bearings. My mother is not in her chair, her white hair peeking above the brown upholstery as I open the door. What am I left holding? Who am I now? Is her acute dependency why I can't let her go?

Holocaust survivor legacy looms like a fog bank on the horizon. The invisible pact I signed onto as part of the family history: to protect her from suffering, to go above and beyond, to assuage past trauma, ameliorate it, and wash it away by doing too much.

Maybe this is why I cannot accept her death. To do so would be to admit I could not protect her from life.

# Unravelling

The cherry wood bowl with the puzzle
fragments, forest scene of deer, fir, lupine,
inches to the lip of the table. I center it near
the stones etched with midnight shapes, a mirage
waiting to come into focus and mean a kind

of solace. I wake in the dark looking for you,
arms outstretched, the invisible baby flying
through the quiet air. I must catch
you, keep you free of suffering,
cradle you back from some brink

that has no name. A sliver of light
like bubbles shimmer in the blackness.
I am puzzling you backward, unmaking the
shape of your mouth, cutting away fragments
in the slow rise to your walker, the glint in

watery, hazel eyes. I am undoing the rough
edges of your laugh clinging to my ceiling.

I want to put down the hollow of my arms, to
smell your momentary presence. I want
to shatter the silence with my
cries and dissolve with you, jagged
pieces that will not fit together.

## You Are Not a Mountain

Orb cloud, slash of pink
in a yin yang molecule

you are not the whole

chartreuse appetite
hushed tones
tiny threads woven
under moonlight

you are not a planet

amidst a galaxy of
unimaginable circles

you are a person person
magenta and blue
layers pulsing through
kaleidoscope stillness

turquoise as an egg
rolling down
a hillside.

# About the Author

Claire Drucker is a Jewish lesbian mom, teacher, poet, and identical twin. Her poems have been published in numerous journals, including *Phoebe, Controlled Burn, Epiphany, Puerto del Sol, Cresset,* and *Women Artists Datebook,* to name a few. Her previous collection of poems, *The Fluid Body,* was published by Finishing Line Press in 2014. Claire lives in Sebastopol, CA, where she's been a longtime English teacher at Santa Rosa Junior College, but now she helps high schoolers find the right college fit as an independent educational consultant. Her passions are dancing, swimming, and hiking with family and friends, as well as communing with pelicans and grey whales off the Pacific coast.

Claire can be reached at:
cdrucker@sonic.net

www.ingramcontent.com/pod-product-compliance
Lightning Source LLC
Chambersburg PA
CBHW022015160426
43197CB00007B/445